**The NABISCO BRANDS Collection of
CREAM of WHEAT Advertising Art**

by David Stivers

Manufactured in the United States of America

First Printing 1986

Library of Congress Number: 86-072123

ISBN 0-917205-04-9

Published and produced by:

Collectors' **SHOWCASE,** *Inc.*

1018 Rosecrans
San Diego, California 92106

Editor: *Donna C. Kaonis*
Design/Art Direction: *D. Keith Kaonis*
Production: *Kathy Johnson*
Typesetting: *Boyer & Brass, San Diego, California*
Color Separations: *Spring Color, San Diego, California*
Printing: *Taylor Publishing, Dallas, Texas*

Front Cover:
"Fifty-Fifty" by Edward Brewer, oil on canvas, 36" × 28", 1923. In this famous illustration, the artist captures the innocence of childhood in a moment of shared intimacy. Cream of Wheat paintings that told a charming story of family love and growing up delighted readers for nearly forty years.

Back Cover:
"Peace and Plenty," by Edward Brewer, oil on canvas, 28" × 22", 1923.

THE NABISCO BRANDS COLLECTION OF

The Nabisco Brands Collection of **Cream of Wheat** ADVERTISING ART

By DAVID STIVERS

A *Collectors'* SHOWCASE
Library Publication

"Financially Embarrassed," oil on canvas, 34" × 24", 1916. Artist/Agency Fee: $250.

CONTENTS

"He Thinks He's So Big," by Haddon Sundblom.
Oil on canvas, 37″ × 34″, 1927. Artist/Agency Fee: $1,035.

INTRODUCTION

Throughout several generations Cream of Wheat has been a favorite of children and adults alike. In the past millions of us have enjoyed the pictorial-style Cream of Wheat advertisements in mass circulation magazines and sang along with the cast of the "Let's Pretend" radio drama, *Cream of Wheat is so good to eat."* Millions more delighted in the adventures of Buck Rogers, and happy to please our mothers, devoured untold boxes of Cream of Wheat in order to acquire the latest premium. And then there were the many years we laughed at the zany adventures of Al Capp's Li'l Abner, spokesman for Cream of Wheat in the '40's and '50's.

How many of us today have an old Cream of Wheat advertisement framed and hanging in the kitchen? The answer is thousands, for their appeal and charming innocence reach out to us, tugging at our heart strings and reminding us of life's simple pleasures.

Beginning around the turn of the century, the Cream of Wheat Company began an advertising campaign that enlisted the talents of America's finest illustrators. Many were just beginning their illustrious careers and they seized upon the opportunity of a lifetime to gain visibility and recognition in the leading magazines of the day.

It is important to remember that prior to the electronic age, magazines were a primary source of entertainment. In those years from the late 1800's to 1930, often termed "The Golden Age" of American illustration, many of our most important artists were hired by companies to illustrate for newspapers, magazines, books and posters.

Under the inspired direction of Emery Mapes, the Cream of Wheat Company commissioned the country's finest illustrators, among them N. C. Wyeth, James Montgomery Flagg, Jessie Willcox Smith, Philip R. Goodwin, J. C. Leyendecker and others.

Many of the Cream of Wheat artists were students of Howard Pyle. Known as the "Father of American Illustration" he is credited with exerting the greatest single influence on those artists of The Golden Age.

If any one theme can be said to dominate this period in art history, it is the representational aspect, an easily understood graphic storytelling that elicited a warm and understanding response in the viewer.

Thus the Cream of Wheat art collection, particularly those paintings dating from the first quarter of this century, reflect the prevalent attitudes and social climate of America's large, emerging middle class during an era of tremendous growth and social change. Paintings are heavily value-laden, creating a romanticized, idyllic view of family life and childhood pleasures.

These are images that recall life's golden moments, touching us with their wholesome appeal and simple innocence. In the early compositions the benevolent chef cleverly appears, sometimes in a subtle soft-selling guise, other times taking center stage. The message is the same; like the hot cereal which brightens a cold, blustery morning, these paintings make the viewer feel warm inside.

By the early fifties, the popularity of television had largely displaced many of the magazines used in the company's advertising campaign. Those remaining often used photographic images in preference to illustrations. The artwork as well as paintings were carefully wrapped, and safely stored away.

In 1962 Cream of Wheat became a part of Nabisco's Grocery Division. In the transition, the paintings, sketches, printer's proofs and premiums were forgotten, each passing year relegating them to a more distant memory.

In 1980 Dave Stivers, archivist at Nabisco Brands and an antique advertising collector in his spare time, located the extensive records that had been maintained for each painting, listing the name of the artist, title, date, purchase price and in what periodicals the ad appeared. Dave traced the artwork to a group of metal lockers in Cream of Wheat's former Minneapolis headquarters. Fortunately the dry, warm heat of the bakery had been excellent for maintaining the paintings. Arranged in chronological order, there were in all about 1600 pieces including original oil on canvas, oil on board, watercolors, sketches, posters, premiums and proofs. The value of the collection which had lain unseen for more than thirty years was appraised in 1980 at over $1,000,000 and, of course, is worth much more today.

Dave enthusiastically began organizing the Cream of Wheat art show, a series of exhibits of the original paintings. During the last few years, groups of forty to fifty paintings have been on loan to various museums, galleries and libraries across the nation.

In the fall of 1985, Dave asked Keith and me to meet with him at Nabisco Brands' East Hanover, New Jersey headquarters to discuss the proposed book on the Cream of Wheat art collection.

A brief tour of the corporate offices showcased many of the original Cream of Wheat paintings. Following our meeting, Dave took us to a storage area where the majority of the paintings and artwork not on loan are stored. Seeing the large bins filled with brown paper wrapped parcels gave me a tiny glimmer of what it must have felt like six years before when Dave opened those dusty lockers in the Minneapolis plant to discover a cache of forgotten art treasures.

The Cream of Wheat art collection is without question one of the most significant art discoveries of this century, documenting not only the advertising history of a company, but providing a charming and meaningful narrative of the styles, manners and mores consciously projected during the early years of the twentieth century.

The fact that such a collection exists at all is remarkable for it was a common practice that commercial artwork remained with the advertising agency, where in a few years time it would likely fall victim to a thorough spring cleaning.

We at *Collectors' SHOWCASE* are extremely grateful for the cooperation and assistance received from Nabisco Brands Archivist Dave Stivers. His boundless enthusiasm, sincere regard and management of this valuable legacy is a tribute to Nabisco Brands. Their desire to share the beauty and enjoyment of this collection has contributed significantly to our understanding and appreciation of "The Golden Age of Illustration." And to the former Cream of Wheat Company we owe a debt of gratitude to those individuals who had the foresight to preserve their company's advertising art, making all of us artistically richer for its existence.

by Donna C. Kaonis co-publisher, Collectors' SHOWCASE

IN THE ARCHIVES

An early
company clock

The author Dave Stivers
spends many happy hours in
the Nabisco Brands archives.
Many of the paintings and
artwork are stored here when
not on exhibit.

Bust of *"The Chef,"* sculpted by
Edward Brewer (pg. 63)

Dave Stivers discovers an original trolley card canvas.

FOREWORD

Mr. Walt Reed

Mr. Walt Reed is a well-known author of books and articles on various artists and aspects of illustration including: *The Illustrator in America 1880–1980; Great American Illustrators; Harold Von Schmidt Draws and Paints The Old West* and *John Clymer, An Artist's Rendezvous with the Frontier West. The Illustrator in America, 1880–1980* by Walt and Roger Reed provided much of the biographical data on the Cream of Wheat artists. Mr. Reed is currently president of Illustration House, Inc., a gallery specializing in the marketing of illustration originals.

The art of advertising has come a long way from the sidewalk hawkers and sandwich boards of a century ago. One of the most important vehicles for this development has been the national magazine, which has evolved along with its advertising.

In the mid-nineteenth century, magazines began to accept small black and white commercial announcements that were relegated to separate back pages. Gradually advertisements grew larger, broke free from the confines of the back section, and colorful illustrations were added to enhance the power of the message. The inside front cover and both sides of the back cover became the most prized, and therefore highest priced, advertising positions. By the turn of the century image quality had improved to the point that artwork by truly fine artists was commissioned and reproduced.

Over the years the growing advertising revenues allowed publishers to increase the number of pages and the quality of their editorial content. The educational benefits reaped by the magazine-reading population through the increase in content quality and quantity would be hard to measure, but there is no doubt that magazines have played a major role in shaping American ideas and attitudes over the past hundred years.

If publishers and the public enjoyed this advantage, the advertisers were also beneficiaries of increased circulation and larger sales volume. By the end of World War I, specialized agencies were developed to practise the art of advertising. Millions of dollars were spent in employing the best artists and copywriters to devise effective ad campaigns and to create corporate identities. Through advertising, art and industry had become partners.

The progress of this development can still be read in back issues of magazines now held in storage racks of public libraries. Rarely, however, is it possible to find the original artwork for an advertiser spanning this whole era. It was unique therefore, to have found the Nabisco collection intact.

To have been in on the discovery of that large cache of more than 500 drawings and paintings was an exciting experience for me as an illustration historian. Locked away in metal storage cabinets in the original plant of Cream of Wheat in Minneapolis and virtually forgotten for several decades, the artwork for advertisements from the turn of the century through the 1940s was all carefully preserved and documented. As the individual items were unwrapped, we found prime examples of artwork by many major illustrators including N. C. Wyeth, Stanley Arthurs, James Montgomery Flagg, J. C. Leyendecker, Maud Tousey Fangel, Haddon Sundblom, and Jessie Willcox Smith. These paintings by stars of illustration history were long believed lost.

To publish this legacy of artwork anew is a unique opportunity, especially to do it from the original paintings and drawings. As one of the most successful and longest-running series of advertising, the Nabisco Brands Cream of Wheat collection provides an historical overview of corporate advertising, and an unparalleled series of excellent paintings resulting from this successful marriage of art and industry.

Feb. 1986

Walt Reed
Illustration House, Inc.

A HISTORY OF CREAM OF WHEAT

Excerpts reprinted from The Story of "Cream of Wheat"

Like many other American institutions, "Cream of Wheat" started in a very small way but with a sound idea and the vision and determination to build a worthwhile business.

One almost-victim of the Panic of 1893 was a small flour mill in Grand Forks, North Dakota, owned and operated by a group of men headed by Emery Mapes, George Bull and George Clifford. These men had fought to keep their milling business alive during the dark days of the Panic and had come through with little operating capital remaining.

About this time, it happened that head miller Tom Amidon was able to sell his partners on the idea of producing for profit a "breakfast porridge" which he had used at home and had found much to his family's liking. Amidon's "porridge" was that part of the wheat taken from the first break rolls of the flour mill. Referred to as "the top of the stream," this is the source of flour of the highest grade. Amidon called it "Cream of Wheat." The partners agreed to let him pack some of this cereal and ship it in a carload of flour going to the firm's New York brokers, Lamont, Corliss & Company.

The funds of the milling company were now so low that Amidon had to cut the cardboard for the cartons by hand, label the packages himself, and crate them in wooden boxes made up from waste lumber. With no money to spend for a package design, Mapes, who had once been a printer, found among his stock of old printing plates a suitable illustration to brighten up the package. It revealed the figure of a black chef holding a saucepan over his shoulder and was the ancestor of the company's present-day widely known trademark.

Within twelve hours after the arrival of the first shipment of "Cream of Wheat" in New York, a telegram was received from Lamont, Corliss saying . . . "Never mind shipping us any more of your flour, but send a carload of "Cream of Wheat."

In 1897 the demand for "Cream of Wheat" had completely outgrown the producing capacity of the small plant at Grand Forks and the business was moved to Minneapolis, then the best source of necessary raw material and a good shipping point with advantageous freight rates to other parts of the country. The original Minneapolis plant was soon

1899 package design for Cream of Wheat.

An early magazine advertisement for Cream of Wheat.

outgrown too, and in 1903 the company moved to a
new building at First Avenue North and Fifth
Street, a familiar Minneapolis landmark which
housed the "Cream of Wheat" plant until 1928.

During these early years, a national
advertising campaign was launched that, considered
a daring innovation at the time with its heavy use
of four color printing, is today even more
remarkable for its rich legacy of illustrative art.
Many of the most famous American artists of the
"Golden Age of Illustration" were commissioned by
the Cream of Wheat Corporation. Happily their
paintings remain not only as examples of fine art
but as a charming reflection of family life during
the early twentieth century.

In 1962 Cream of Wheat became a part of
Nabisco's Grocery Division. At that time Nabisco
was known as the National Biscuit Company, a title
that changed in 1971 to Nabisco and to Nabisco
Brands in 1981 when the company merged with
Standard Brands.

Throughout the years, Cream of Wheat has
maintained its position as one of the nation's
leading hot breakfast cereals. "Regular" Cream of
Wheat is the same nutritious product that has been
a standby in homes for over ninety years. "Quick,"
"Instant" and "Mix 'n Eat" Cream of Wheat were
gradually added, providing consumers on the run a
healthful, hot breakfast.

CREAM OF WHEAT ILLUSTRATORS

Harry Anderson
Stanley M. Arthurs
H. S. Benton
E. B. Bird
Helen Blackburn
M. L. Blumenthal
M. Leone Bracker
Worth Brehm
E. V. Brewer
Mabel Buckmaster
William V. Cahill
Charles Champe
Walter Appleton Clark
Osgood Cochi
Arthur Crisp
Maud Tousey Fangel
Denman Fink
James Montgomery Flagg
Alan Foster
Philip R. Goodwin
Norman T. Hall
Edwin Henry
Frank B. Hoffman
John Newton Howitt
August W. Hutaf
Henry Hutt
B. Corey Kilvert
Harry B. Lachman
Loyd L. LaDriere

Joseph Christian Leyendecker
Andrew Loomis
Philip Lyford
Mac Martin
Helen Mason
Frederick Kimball Mizen
Galen G. Perrett
John Rae
Henry Patrick Raleigh
Fletcher Ransom
Otto Schneider
John G. Scott
Jessie Willcox Smith
Rowland M. Smith
Roy Frederic Spreter
Alice Barber Stephens
James Reeve Stuart
Haddon Hubbard Sundblom
Leslie Thrasher
Frank Verbeck
Leslie Wallace
Ernest Watson
Walter Whitehead
C. G. Widney
Robert Wildhack
Harry F. Wireman
Katherine Richardson Wireman
Newell Convers Wyeth
Florence Wyman

Continued research may reveal additional artists.

"Old King Cole," 1902. Unknown artist.

THE ART OF CREAM OF WHEAT

In 1902 the Cream of Wheat Company appropriated its first advertising budget of $10,000—a budget that was to increase steadily over the years.

During his lifetime, Emery Mapes set the advertising policies, commissioned the artwork and even wrote much of the copy. The routine job of purchasing advertising space and coordinating placement was largely done by the advertising agency of J. Walter Thompson.

As an art lover and an advertising genius, Mapes made an enormous contribution to the maturing status of artists hired to illustrate for the leading advertisers of the day.

The earliest paintings used in Cream of Wheat advertisements are not signed, but as commercial art gained recognition and respect, the Cream of Wheat illustrations proudly bear the signatures of many illustrious *"Golden Age"* artists whose works are outstanding examples of this period in art history.

A three inch ad, *(below)* the first for the Cream of Wheat Company, appeared in the November 1896 issue of the *Ladies' Home Journal.* A modified version appeared again in 1897.

"We'll make him eyes
And we'll make him a nose
But without feet he can't have toes.
We'll ask mamma for a frying pan
And make his cap the best we can
He'll be a man *that can't be beat*
And look like the one on

Cream of Wheat

Cream of Wheat Co.   Minneapolis Minn.

CREAM of WHEAT supplies nutritive material in such abundance that children fed on it are splendidly robust, feeling neither extreme of cold nor heat.

ASK THE GROCER FOR OUR ELEGANT VIEWS OF NORTHWEST SCENERY, ENTIRELY WITHOUT ADVERTISING MARK.

"Among Childhood Pleasures," black and white gouache, 11″ × 7½″. Harper's Magazine, 1900. Unknown artist.

HAVE YOU TRIED THE NEW Breakfast FOOD ?

Cream of Wheat

s not only one of the most delicate and de- us breakfast dishes, but being composed ost entirely of pure gluten is especially mmended for persons of weak digestion.

THE NORTH DAKOTA MILLING CO.

Sole Manuf'rs, Grand Forks, N. D.

HMAN BROS., 78 Hudson St., New York, Agts. d *for sample package, and 200-page cook book, free.*

HAVE YOU TRIED THE NEW Breakfast FOOD ?

Cream of Wheat

It is not only one of the most delicate and deli- cious breakfast dishes, but being composed almost entirely of pure gluten, is especially recommended

FOR PERSONS OF WEAK DIGESTION

The North Dakota Milling Co., Sole Manuf'rs **Grand Forks, N. Dak.**

CUSHMAN BROS. CO., 78 HUDSON ST., NEW YORK, AGENTS Sample and 200-page cook-book, free, if you mention this magazine

The Cream of Wheat illustrations appeared as magazine ads in the leading periodicals of the time. These included: *The Saturday Evening Post, Good Housekeeping, Woman's Home Companion, Youth's Companion, McCall's, Pictorial Review, Red Book, Delineator-Designer, Modern Priscilla, Munsey's, Literary Digest, National Geographic, Colliers* and others. Many of these publications are no longer in existence.

The artist/agency fee *(see photo captions)* is the original price paid for the illustration. Any subsequent fees paid for modifications or revisions are not included in this figure.

Among Life's Pleasures

A picnic luncheon is apt to be so disappointing, and it's such a labor to prepare. The sandwiches get soggy, the cakes break, everything is stuffy by the time you get where you want to go. Why not take a little kettle, a bottle of cream, a few small bowls and a package of

Cream of Wheat?

The woods furnish your gypsy fire, the brook, clear running water, and in a few moments you have a meal so dainty and delicious, fresh and appetizing, as to add charm to the sylvan surroundings.

A coupon will be found in every package of Cream of Wheat. Send us ten of these coupons and ten cents and we will send you free, your choice of three beautiful pictures, described more fully in the coupon referred to.

CREAM OF WHEAT CO., Minneapolis, Minn.

"Among Life's Pleasures," photo montage, black and white wash, 14″ × 11″. *Harper's Magazine*, 1900. Unknown artist.

Christmas Pleasures.

The mistletoe hung on the chandelier
And he kissed her there with never a fear,
For the soup was delicious, the turkey fine,
The pudding was rich, the sauce divine,
And then came the fruits and confections so sweet
But none of them better than Cream of Wheat.

CREAM OF WHEAT
MEETS EVERY REQUIREMENT OF THE GROWING BODY, AND SUPPLIES THE WASTE OF AGE; IT IS BRAIN AND MUSCLE FOOD, AS IT IS CHIEFLY GLUTEN AND PHOSPHATES.

CREAM OF WHEAT CO., Minneapolis, Minn.

"Fate Cannot Harm Me, I Have Dined To-day."

This expresses the feeling of a man who has eaten Cream of Wheat. It is a food that is both good to eat and "good for you." That is what Cream of Wheat is.
A Dainty Breakfast Dish. Delicious Desserts.

Cream of Wheat

Far left:
"Christmas Pleasures," black & white, line and wash, 12″ × 8″. *American Monthly*, 1900. Unknown artist.

Left:
"Fate Cannot Harm Me," opaque watercolor, 1902. Unknown artist.

Opposite:
Chef at Masquerade, opaque watercolor, 16″ × 11″, 1901. Unknown artist.

Among Life's Pleasures

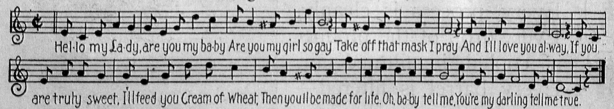

Hel-lo my La-dy, are you my ba-by Are you my girl so gay Take off that mask I pray And I'll love you al-way, If you

are truly sweet, I'll feed you Cream of Wheat; Then you'll be made for life. Oh, ba-by tell me, You're my darling tell me true.

Cream of Wheat!

Rich in gluten and phosphates is the most appetiz-ing and invigorating of all cereal foods

With each purchase of two packages your grocer gives you an elegant gravure of Northwestern Scenery 15×17 inches, mounted without mark of any kind.

CREAM OF WHEAT CO. MINNEAPOLIS, MINN.

Harvest Scene, line and wash, 12″ × 8″, 1901.
Artist/Agency Fee: $150. Unknown artist.

Opposite:
"Mistress Mary, Quite Contrary," 1902.
Unknown artist.

MISTRESS MARY, QUITE CONTRARY,
HOW DOES YOUR GARDEN GROW?
WITH WHEAT SO NEAT,
AND CREAM SO SWEET,
AND POSIES ALL IN A ROW.

THE BEST AND DAINTIEST CEREAL FOOD CREAM OF WHEAT
IS SOLD BY GROCERS EVERYWHERE.
CREAM OF WHEAT CO. MINNEAPOLIS, MINN.

18

TO MARKET,
  TO MARKET.
TO BUY
CREAM of WHEAT
HOME AGAIN,
  HOME AGAIN,
DANCE DOWN THE STREET.

CREAM of WHEAT IS THE BEST AND DAINTIEST CEREAL FOOD
SOLD BY GROCERS EVERYWHERE.
CREAM of WHEAT CO. MINNEAPOLIS, MINN.

"To Market, To Market," 1902. Unknown artist.

"To the Summer Girl," 1904. Unknown artist. Notice the white areas outlining the chef's pot and the woman's head. This indicates modifications to the original illustration in preparation for photo copying.

"The Autocrat of the Breakfast Table," opaque watercolor, 16″ × 10½″. Unknown artist.

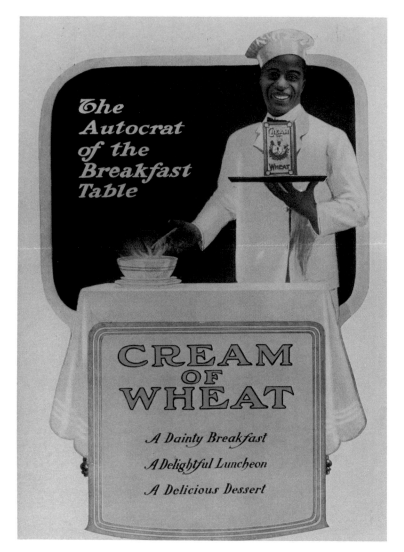

"Resolved for 1904," black and white photo montage. Unknown artist.

"Mother's Favorite," 1905. Unknown artist.

"Children Everywhere," black and white wash, 23″ × 17½″, 1906. Unknown artist.

"Santa Claus Christmas Breakfast," watercolor, 15″ × 17″, 1906. Unknown artist.

"A New Arrival at Palm Beach,"
Photo collage, 28″ × 21¼″,
1911. Unknown artist.

Henry Hutt
1875–1950

"A Dainty Breakfast," opaque watercolor, 34″ × 23½″, 1906.

Born in Chicago, Illinois, Hutt studied at the Chicago Art Institute. He sold his first picture to the old *Life* magazine at the age of sixteen and thereafter illustrated for most of the magazines of his day.

In a day when the illustrators set the fashion, no artist was more influential in depicting the stylish, up-to-date female than Henry Hutt. The *Henry Hutt Picture Book,* a volume containing more than eighty of his illustrations, published by the Century Company, was a popular gift book in 1908.

Philip R. Goodwin
1882–1935

"A Bear Chance," oil on board,
14¾" × 9¼", 1908.
Artist/Agency Fee: $175.

Philip R. Goodwin of Norwich, Connecticut,
was a student at the Rhode Island School of Design
and Art Students League in New York. He also
studied with Howard Pyle. His work exhibits much
of Pyle's earnestness and discipline but is restricted
almost entirely to subjects of hunting and fishing.
In this limited area, however, he produced many
notable pictures, the subject matter always being
convincing and dramatic in color.

"Our Platform," oil on board,
26″ × 20½″, 1908.
Artist/Agency Fee: $62.50.

Our Platform

Cream of Wheat

A dainty breakfast
A delicious luncheon
A delightful dessert

Harry Stacy Benton

Born 1877. Painter and illustrator.
Attended Chicago Art Institute.

B. Corey Kilvert
1881–1946

Illustrator of children's books.
Employed at *Collier's,*
New York World.

"Lest We Forget," opaque watercolor, 23″ × 17″, 1907. Artist/Agency Fee: $300.

Otto J. Schneider

"Raised on Cream of Wheat," 1907.

Portrait painter, etcher and illustrator. Member of Chicago Society of Etchers. Born in Atlanta, Illinois, 1875. Represented in Art Institute of Chicago; also by portraits of Lincoln, McKinley, Emerson and Mark Twain.

"The Pirate,"
pencil and watercolor,
18″ × 13″, 1907.

Florence Wyman

N. C. Wyeth
1882–1945

Newell Convers Wyeth was born in rural Massachusetts in 1882. In 1899 Wyeth graduated from the Mechanic Arts School in Boston where he had studied drafting. He continued his education at the Massachusetts Normal Art School and later the Eric Pape School of Art in Boston. In 1902 Wyeth went to Wilmington to study with Howard Pyle. Shortly after, his famous painting of a bronco buster was used as a cover for the *Saturday Evening Post.*

In 1906 the young Wyeth wrote to his mother regarding his work for The Cream of Wheat Company: "Mr. Mapes of the Cream of Wheat Co. telegraphed for me to run up and see him at the Waldorf-Astoria. He is the owner of that famous cereal company and is a man of immense wealth. I have just completed two pictures for him, $250 each, which he is immensely pleased with." Wyeth is referring to "Where the Mail Goes Cream of Wheat Goes" and "The Bronco Buster," two well-known illustrations that appeared for several months on the inside front cover of the leading magazines of the day.

His third painting for Cream of Wheat, "The Yukon Freighter," Wyeth described as a "whopper," probably referring to its five by three foot size.

Wyeth emulated Pyle's approach as nearly as possible, adding his own dramatic picture concepts and rich decorative color.

He illustrated many of the great fiction classics including *Treasure Island, Robin Hood* and *Robinson Crusoe.* Later in his career, he began to paint more landscapes and scenes of the countryside and Maine coast.

Wyeth's children were encouraged to develop their talents. Andrew, Carolyn and Henriette became famous artists, another daughter, Ann, studied music and his son Nathaniel, engineering. N. C. Wyeth died in 1945.

"Where The Mail Goes Cream of Wheat Goes," 1908.

Opposite:
e Yukon Freighter,"
oil on canvas,
40″ × 35″, 1908.
Artist/Agency Fee:
$500.

"The Bronco Buster," 1907. Artist/Agency Fee: $500.

M. L. Blumenthal

Moses Laurence Blumenthal was born in 1879 in Wilmington, North Carolina. He was a student at the Pennsylvania Museum School. Moses illustrated for many of the leading magazines of the day: *The Saturday Evening Post, The Ladies' Home Journal, Collier's, McClure's* and *Scribner's.*

"When the Wish,"
watercolor, 7″ × 5″, 1911.
Artist/Agency Fee: $100.

"Stingy-Stingy," opaque watercolor, 28″ × 19″, 1912. Artist/Agency Fee: $100.

Alice Barber
Stephens
1858–1932

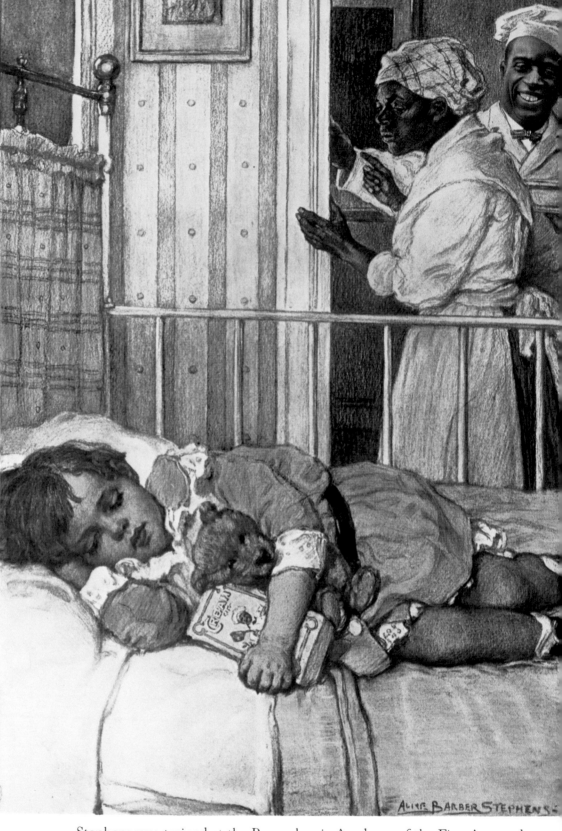

"Fast Asleep," charcoal and watercolor, 27½″ × 18¼″, 1908.

Stephens was trained at the Pennsylvania Academy of the Fine Arts and at the Philadelphia School of Design for Women, where she later taught portrait and life classes.

Sincerity and good taste, as well as her technical excellence, make the illustrations of Alice Barber Stephens a pleasure to look at. The early discipline of her work as a wood engraver for *Scribner's* was in some measure responsible for her fine draftsmanship. She was most successful in quiet settings, with humble subjects—among her best is a series of pictures of old men and women, inmates of the Philadelphia almshouse.

John Newton Howitt

W. V. Cahill

Over a period of several years, Cahill did eighteen paintings for Cream of Wheat. He was a student of Howard Pyle. Works include: "Thoughts of the Sea," in the Museum of History, Science and Art, Los Angeles, and "Summer," Municipal Collection, Phoenix, Arizona. Cahill died in 1924.

"In the Good Old Summer Time," opaque, 30½" × 20", 1905.

Oppos *"Building With Blocks,"* oil on canv 36" × 26", 1910. Artist/Agency Fee: $5

W.V.CAHILL

"Don't Forget Cream of Wheat,"
oil on canvas, 35″ × 20″, 1910.
Artist/Agency Fee: $500.

"The Cooking Lesson,"
oil on canvas, 36″ × 26″, 1910.
Artist/Agency Fee: $500.

"Breakfast's Ready," oil on canvas, 36″ × 26″, 1913. Artist/Agency Fee: $300.

"A Sign of Good Living," opaque watercolor, 35½″ × 24½″, 1911. Artist/Agency Fee: $150.

W. V. Cahill

"Look Pleasant Please," oil on canvas, 36″ × 28″, 1914. Artist/Agency Fee: $250.

Opposite: *"Frost Pictures,"* oil on canvas, 36″ × 26″, 1911.

J. C. Leyendecker
1874–1951

Born in Montabour, Germany, Joseph Christian Leyendecker and his family moved to Chicago when he was eight years old. Showing great promise at an early age, he attended evening classes at the Art Institute of Chicago. He and his brother Frank continued their education at the Academie Julien in France.

Upon their return two years later, Leyendecker had no difficulty in obtaining top commissions for advertising illustrations and cover designs for the leading publications. His first *Post* cover was done in 1899 and over the next forty years, he did well over 300 more. Among the most famous of these was the annual New Year baby series.

One of Leyendecker's most popular creations was the handsome, debonair Arrow Collar man. His illustrations for Hart, Schaffner & Marx were equally successful in promoting an image of suited elegance.

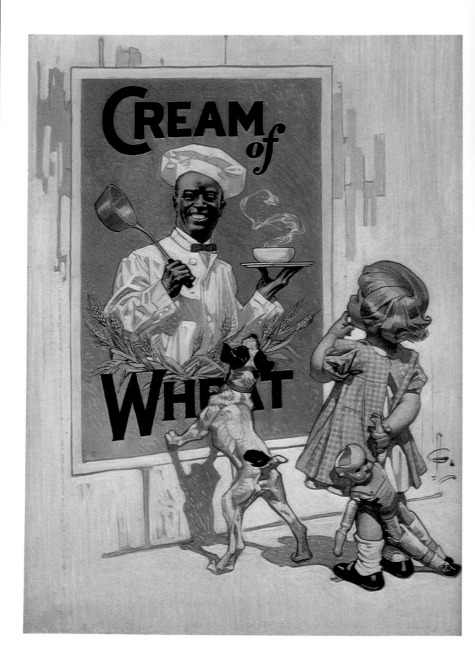

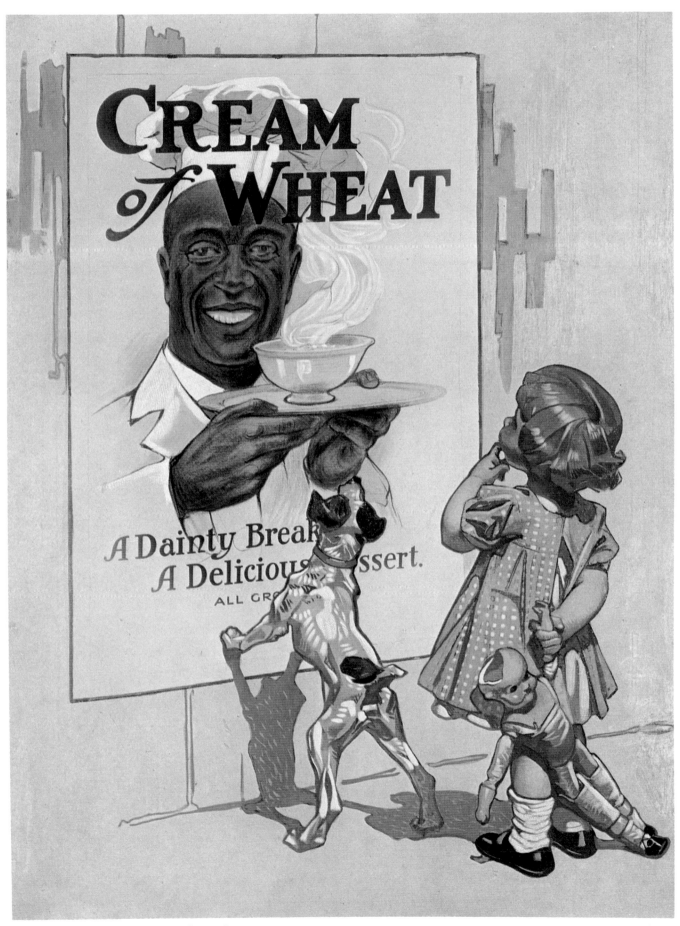

"A Dainty Breakfast," oil on canvas, 30" × 22", 1909.
The 1920 modification by Brewer is pictured on the facing page.
Artist/Agency Fee: $150.

George Gibbs

Painter and illustrator.
Born in New Orleans,
Louisiana, 1870.
Pupil of Corcoran
School of Art.

"In the Dining Car,"
opaque watercolor, 20″ × 14″, 1907.
Artist/Agency Fee: $200.

"Cream of Wheat is Ready," watercolor, 20″ × 13″, 1909.

James Montgomery Flagg
1877–1960

James Montgomery Flagg epitomized the public concept of the handsome bohemian artist surrounded by beautiful models. He worked rapidly and easily in all media and with any subject matter. Humor and satire were his special forte and his rapid portrait studies and incisive caricatures were prized by many prominent sitters.

For over 30 years he turned out an immense amount of work, including many posters during World War I. Probably his best known illustration was the famous "I Want You" Uncle Sam recruiting poster of which over four million copies were printed and distributed throughout the country.

Stanley Massey Arthurs
1877-1950

Stanley Massey Arthurs was a student and close personal friend of Howard Pyle. He devoted his career to depicting American historical subjects, painting a series of episodes from earliest colonial times through the Civil War era.

Arthurs' use of color was rich and varied. Many of his illustrations are reproduced in James Truslow Adams' *History of the United States,* in the 15-volume *Pageant of America* edited by Ralph H. Gabriel, and in *The American Historical Scene* published by the University of Pennsylvania Press in 1935.

Arthurs also painted a number of murals including the "Landing of DeVries" at Delaware College and "The Crusaders" at the State Capitol, Dover, Delaware. Note: The work of Susan Arthurs is believed by many to be the work of Stanley Arthurs.

"A Visit with the Chef,"
oil on board, 27" × 23", 1911.

Opposite:
"School Days,"
oil on canvas, 36" × 24", 1908.
Artist/Agency Fee: $200.

Jessie Willcox Smith
1863–1935

Throughout her long career, Jessie Willcox Smith specialized in drawing and painting mothers, babies and children. She worked primarily with charcoal, watercolor and gouache while supplementing her substantial income with commissioned oil portraits of children. Her training was acquired at the School of Design for Women, the Pennsylvania Academy of the Fine Arts with Thomas Eakins, and at the Drexel Institute under Howard Pyle.

She had first planned to be a kindergarten teacher but turned to an art career with the stimulus and assistance of Howard Pyle. Some of her best-known illustrations were for books: *Little Women, Heidi, A Book of Old Stories,* and Robert Louis Stevenson's *A Child's Garden of Verses.* She also painted a great many illustrations for leading magazines such as *McClure's, Scribner's, Woman's Home Companion* and *Good Housekeeping,* for which she did nearly 200 covers.

She painted and exhibited widely, receiving many awards, including a Silver Medal at the Panama-Pacific Exposition at San Francisco in 1915.

Opposite:
"I Know that Man,"
charcoal and watercolor, 20" × 18", 1909.
Artist/Agency Fee: $416.

CREAM of WHEAT

JESSIE WILLCOX SMITH.

C. G. Widney

"Fe Fi Fo Fum,"
collage and watercolor, 16″ × 20″, 1909.
Artist/Agency Fee: $199.50

Opposite:
"King Arthur,"
opaque watercolor, 16″ × 20″, 1910.
Artist/Agency Fee: $250

When Good King Arthur ruled the land,
He was a goodly King:
He stole three pecks of barley meal
To make a bag pudding.

A bag pudding the Queen did make
And stuffed it well with plums;
And put therein great lumps of fat
As big as my two thumbs.

The King and Queen did eat thereof
And all the Court beside;
And what they could not eat that night
The Queen next morning fried.

When next the King did feast his Court
He spread a royal board;
Nor plums nor fat was served thereat
To tempt each Dame and Lord.

Yet when the Queen arose next morn
There was naught left to fry,
Whereat she sat upon a stool
And piteously did cry.

Of all that mighty feast was left
No single scrap to eat.
All had been valiant trencher-men,
For 'twas the **Cream of Wheat.**

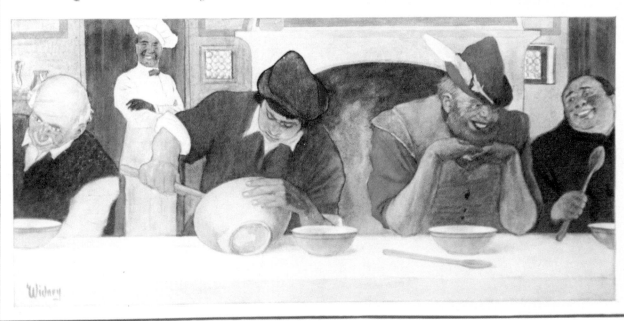

Walter Whitehead
1874–1956

Walter Whitehead was born in
Chicago, Illinois in 1874. He studied
at the Art Institute of Chicago before
joining the Howard Pyle School of Art
about 1901. Whitehead later returned
to Chicago and eventually taught at
the Chicago Academy of Fine Arts.

"Encore,"
oil on canvas, 31″ × 20″, 1910.
Artist/Agency Fee: $100.

Opposite:
"Poor Old Robinson Crusoe,"
also titled *"Buried Treasure,"*
oil on canvas, 36″ × 26″, 1909.
Artist/Agency Fee: $135.

Charles Champe

"Winter Scene," opaque watercolor,
21¼" × 14¾", 1911.

"In The Gloaming,"
oil on canvas, 25″ × 18″, 1912.
Artist/Agency Fee: $200.

Helen Mason

Denman Fink
1881-1956

Denman Fink was born in 1881 in Springdale, PA. He was educated at the Pittsburgh School of Design and the Boston Museum of Art. At the age of nineteen, Fink became an illustrator for *Scribner's,* later working for *Harper's,* the *Saturday Evening Post* and other well-known publications of the day.

In 1924 Denman Fink moved to the Miami area where he worked as the head of the art department at the University of Miami for twenty-five years until his retirement.

Although nationally known and recognized as an illustrator, portrait artist and muralist, Fink received his greatest acclaim for his designs for Coral Gables, Florida. His magnificent entrances, fountains, pools and landscaped streets brought physical beauty to an entire city.

"The Glutton,"
oil on canvas, 30″ × 21″, 1909.
Artist/Agency Fee: $200.

Opposite:
"Anticipation," oil on canvas,
23″ × 16″, 1911.

Fletcher Ransom

"Country Life in America," oil on canvas, 20″ × 28″, 1911.
Artist/Agency Fee: $200.

"Country Life in America," oil on canvas, 20" × 28", 1910.

"Old Santa Knows,"
watercolor, 14″ × 12″, 1912.
Note the Chef in the earlier
painting (above) in a full-face
position. In the later painting, the
head has been retouched and
turned at an angle.

E. B. Bird
1867-1943

Well-known poster artist during the twenties and
thirties.

"A Proud Day for Rastus,"
oil on canvas, 40″ × 28″, 1914.
Artist/Agency Fee: $250.

The chef was prominently featured in many of the early Cream of Wheat advertisements. Until Brewer sculpted a bust of the chef, the popular character was depicted only full face. A three dimensional model allowed Brewer to paint the chef in a variety of poses. Brewer's 1914 painting, *"A Proud Day for Rastus,"* is a self-portrait of the artist executing the sculpture of the chef.

A versatile artist, Brewer sculpted this bust, thus enabling him to paint the Chef from various angles.

Edward V. Brewer
1883–1971

For a period of several years beginning in 1911 until 1926, the work of Minnesota born Edward Brewer dominated the Cream of Wheat advertisements; in all 102 paintings are attributed to him.

Ed Brewer grew up in an atmosphere dedicated to painting and was greatly encouraged in his early endeavors to become an artist. His father Nicholas Brewer was also a painter of considerable repute, who during his lifetime was commissioned by several nationally prominent figures.

As a youth, Edward Brewer found little satisfaction in the various clerical positions he was forced to accept. Painting in his off hours, he eventually realized a small profit from his work, and thus was able to devote his full time to artistic pursuits.

Prior to working on the Cream of Wheat account, Brewer had several other clients including Abercrombie & Fitch and *Field and Stream* magazine where he soon became art editor.

His first ad for Cream of Wheat was published in 1911. According to Brewer, Emery Mapes told him he wished to patronize a local artist rather than hire leading illustrators elsewhere.

In 1914 Brewer appeared in one of his own paintings entitled "A Proud Day for Rastus." The picture is a self portrait of the artist sculpting a clay bust of the black chef. Brewer did in fact make such a bust as evidenced by the sculpture made from his original mold.

In all previous Cream of Wheat paintings, the chef had been drawn full face, however, now with a three-dimensional model, Brewer began to paint the chef from various angles.

Brewer's style has often been compared to the work of Norman Rockwell. Drawing on familiar surroundings, family and friends, his paintings capture the innocence of childhood and the traditional values of family life.

Brewer often used his own studio decorated with antique furnishings as a backdrop for his paintings. His three children were frequently employed as models. In one of his best known works, the 1919 "Mighty Oaks from Tiny Acorns Grow," his son David posed for the sad-faced newspaper boy sitting with his dog in front of a statue of Lincoln.

The work of other well-known artists was retained by The Cream of Wheat Corporation after 1926 and Brewer went on to paint for a number of other clients. For some twenty years starting in the early 1940's, he was commissioned by the Jensen Printing Company of Minneapolis to do their annual calendar paintings.

"Say Cream of Wheat,"
oil on canvas, 40″ × 28″, 1915.
Artist/Agency Fee: $250.

E. V. Brewer

"Ali Baba and the Forty Thieves," oil on canvas, 40″ × 28″, 1914. Artist/Agency Fee: $250.

E. V. Brewer

"Rip Van Winkle,"
oil on canvas, 40″ × 28″, 1915.
Artist/Agency Fee: $250.

"Mighty Oaks From Tiny Acorns Grow," 1919. One of Brewer's last and finest paintings was this poignant portrayal of his son David dressed as a newsboy. It was the personal favorite of Brewer's wife, and during the last years of her life Brewer requested that it be returned. The picture was returned to the artist and it remains in the Brewer family to this day.

68

E. V. Brewer

"He Sho' Thinks He's Hiding,"
oil on canvas,
34″ × 24″, 1916.

Opposite:
"Circus Day," oil on canvas,
34″ × 24″, 1916.
Artist/Agency Fee: $250.

Tool →

Tool

Tool

gnettes
e original

CREAM of WHEAT

PERFORMANCE
EVERY MORNING
AT 7:00
EVERY NIGHT
AT 6:00

EX

EDW. V. BREWER

"In His Father's Footsteps," **oil on canvas, 40" × 30", 1924. Artist/Agency Fee: $375.**

E. V. Brewer

"Playing Store," oil on canvas, 40″ × 28″,
1915. Artist/Agency Fee: $250.

E. V. Brewer

"Here You Are,"
oil on canvas, 34″ × 24″, 1917.
Artist/Agency Fee: $250.

"Standing Back of Uncle Sam,"
oil on canvas, 34" × 24",
1918. Artist/Agency Fee: $250.

"The Best Policy," oil on board, 25″ × 17″, 1922. Artist/Agency Fee: $300.

"Keeping Watch," oil on canvas, *26″ × 20″,* 1922.

"Passed by the Board," oil on canvas, 37" × 28", 1923. Artist/Agency Fee: $300.

"Well Fortified," oil on canvas, 36" × 28", 1923. Artist/Agency Fee: $375.

E. V. Brewer

"Starting the New Year Right,"
oil on canvas, 25″ × 20″, 1923. Artist/Agency Fee: $300.

"Getting Up Steam," oil on canvas, 30" × 25", 1924.

E. V. Brewer

"The Two Best Friends," oil on canvas, 30½″ × 19″, 1922.

"Right Over The Home Plate," oil on canvas, 37" × 28", 1923.

"Some Like It Hot," oil on canvas, 34″ × 26″, 1924.   *Opposite: "From Sunrise to Twilight,"* oil on canvas, 26″ × 21″, 1924.

"*Counting His Pennies*," oil on canvas, 36″ × 30″, 1924. Artist/Agency Fee: $450.

Opposite: "*The Order of the Day*," 30″ × 22″, 1924.

E. V. Brewer

"Mental Fatigue," oil on canvas,
21″ × 27″, 1924.

"Little Engines That Burn,"
oil on canvas, 32″ × 36″, 1924.
Artist/Agency Fee: $400.

"The Makings of a Man," oil on canvas, 25″ × 21″, 1924.

E. V. Brewer

"Laying the Corner Stone," oil on canvas, 34″ × 25″, 1924. Artist/Agency Fee: $375.

"A Good Start is Half the Journey," oil on canvas, 26″ × 20″, 1926. Artist/Agency Fee: $450.

A GOOD START IS HALF THE JOURNEY

Charles Leslie Thrasher
1889-1936

Leslie Thrasher was born in Piedmont, West Virginia. He studied at the Pennsylvania Academy of the Fine Arts and later studied under Howard Pyle.

Thrasher was best known for his humorous covers done for the *Saturday Evening Post* and *Liberty* magazines. His first published cover was sold to the *Saturday Evening Post* in 1912 for $50.00. By 1926 he had contracted to do a cover a week for *Liberty* at $1,000.00 each. These covers constituted a series which depicted the life of a "typical American family," in the words of *Liberty* editors. The model used for the likeness of the father was Thrasher. The story told by the covers was made into a feature-length movie called *For Love of Lil.*

In addition to covers, Thrasher did story illustrations and ads, some of which became quite well known. These appeared in such magazines as *Everybody's, Collier's, Red Book, Popular Magazine,* and others. His prodigious output was consistently lighthearted and painted in an accomplished style full of sparkle and vitality.

Opposite:
"Playing Hooky,"
oil on canvas, 36" × 24", 1912.
Artist/Agency Fee: $250.

"Our Platform," oil on canvas, 36″ × 24″, 1913. Artist/Agency Fee: $250.

Galen J. Perrett

Born in Chicago in 1875. Pupil of Chicago Art Institute and of the Julien Academy, Paris.

"Preparedness,"
oil on canvas, 30" × 24",
1917.

"Well, You're Helping Some,"
oil on canvas, 18" × 26", 1915.
Artist/Agency Fee: $100.

G. G. Perrett

"Mary Ann You Can Just Wait," oil on canvas, 34″ × 26″, 1913. Artist/Agency Fee: $100.

MARY ANN!
*You can
just* WAIT.

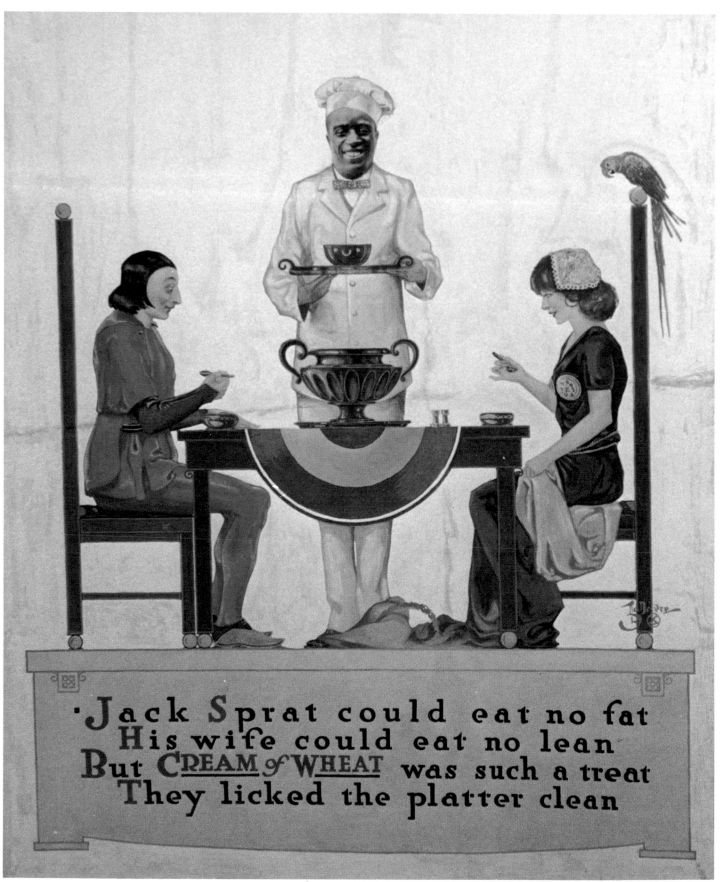

"Jack Sprat," opaque watercolor, 32" × 26", 1915.

John Scott

John Scott was born in Camden, New Jersey in 1907. He is best known for his wildlife illustrations depicting hunting and fishing scenes.

ALL THE RICHES
   OF WHICH WE BOAST,
TIS CREAM OF WHEAT
   WE TREASURE MOST;
THE DIAMONDS AND JEWELS
   WE HAND TO OUR WIVES,
BUT CREAM OF WHEAT
   WE GUARD WITH OUR LIVES.

"The Treasure Chest," opaque watercolor,
28″ × 20″, 1924. Artist/Agency Fee: $150.

"The Spirit of 1924," opaque watercolor, 23″ × 18″, 1924.

James Leslie Wallace

Top left:
"One Sweetly Solemn Thought,"
watercolor, 15½" × 11", 1910.
Artist/Agency Fee: $100.

Top right:
"What Do I Care,"
opaque watercolor,
17½" × 12¼", 1913.
Artist/Agency Fee: $100.

Right: "To Market, To Market,"
watercolor, 25¼" × 18¼",
1916. Artist/Agency Fee: $100.

"Cream of Wheat Can't Be Beat," watercolor, 17″ × 14″, 1926.

Katharine Richardson Wireman

1878-1966

Katharine Richardson was born in Philadelphia in 1878. She studied with Howard Pyle at Drexel in 1899, and then lived in Germantown as part of the close-knit group of women who studied with Pyle and then pursued careers in illustration. She did illustrations, including covers, for *Country Gentlemen, Scribner's, Ladies' Home Journal, Saturday Evening Post,* and *Collier's.*

"Cream of Wheat for Sail," oil on canvas, 18″ × 24″, 1912. Artist/Agency Fee: $250.

K. R. Wireman

"Bringing Home the Holly," oil on canvas, 22″ × 28″, 1914. Artist/Agency Fee: $250.

Harry F. Wireman

"Saying Grace," opaque watercolor, 25″ × 16″, 1917. It is interesting to note that this charming painting incorporates two other Cream of Wheat paintings by different artists.

Frank B. Hoffman
1888-1958

"A Model Diet," oil on board, 22″ × 25½″, 1924.
Artist/Agency Fee: $356.

Frank Hoffman was born in Chicago into a family which had once been prominent Ohio landowners and horsebreeders. His father's interest in thoroughbred racing may have been responsible for Frank's knowledge of horses and his ability to depict them so well. Charles M. Russell once remarked that "Nobody can draw a horse like Hoffman."

Early in his career Hoffman worked for the *Chicago American* where he eventually became head of the art department.

In 1916 Hoffman moved west where he finally settled in Taos, New Mexico. His bold, broad brush work and striking color attracted the attention of advertisers. He painted for national campaigns for many corporations, including Great National Railroad, General Motors and General Electric. This was followed by illustrations for several national magazines for which he specialized in Western subjects.

From 1940 on, Hoffman was under exclusive contract to Brown and Bigelow and painted over 150 canvases of the West which were used as calendar subjects.

"The Age of Thrills," oil on canvas, 25″ × 30″, 1924.

F. B. Hoffman

"Serious Business," oil on canvas, *21″ × 21″*, 1923.
Artist/Agency Fee: $1,150.

John Rae
1882-1963

A student of Howard Pyle, Rae also attended the Art Students League of New York. He was a prolific writer and illustrator of children's books; one of his best known works was *The New Adventures of Alice,* a continuation of the original Lewis Carroll story.

During his lifetime, Rae painted portraits of such well known personalities as Albert Einstein, Carl Sandburg, opera singer Freda Hempel, and composer Harold V. Milligan.

"It's a Busy World,"
oil on canvas,
16" × 21", 1925.
Artist/Agency
Fee: $1,150.

"Eat Wisely & Keep Cool," opaque watercolor, 17" × 18", 1925.

Maud Tousey Fangel
1881-1968

Maud Tousey Fangel is best known for her beautifully rendered paintings of children. Much of her work was done in pastels, appropriate to her subjects in range of color and softness of texture.

For many years she was very productive as a cover designer for the *Ladies' Home Journal, McCall's, Woman's Home Companion,* and many other magazines, as well as an illustrator for several national products. She was also a well known doll designer.

Born in Boston, Mrs. Fangel attended the Massachusetts Normal Art School, Cooper Union, and the Art Students League in New York. She died in 1968 at the age of 87.

"Baby's Second Summer," pastel, 27″ × 21″, 1925.

"Your Baby Needs," pastel, 15″ × 14″, 1924. Artist/Agency Fee: $1,150.

"The Important Business,"
pastel, 19″ × 18″, 1924.
Artist/Agency Fee: $1,150.

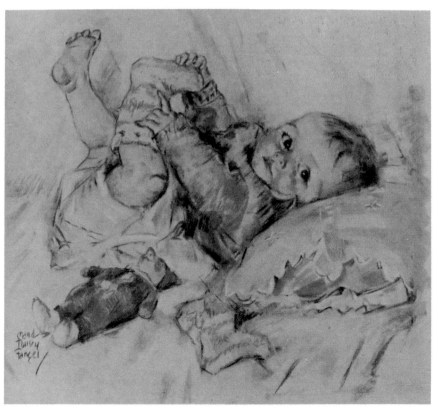

"Who's Busier Than a Baby,"
pastel, 18½″ × 20¾″, 1925.
Artist/Agency Fee: $1,150.

Frederic Kimball Mizen
1888-1965

Mizen was a dominant figure in the outdoor advertising field. He also did fiction illustration for magazines such as *Cosmopolitan* and *The Saturday Evening Post*, but is probably best known for his long and distinguished series of advertising paintings for the Coca-Cola Company in newspapers, magazines, and billboards.

"In High Gear," oil on canvas, 24″ × 28″, 1926. Artist/Agency Fee: $747.50.

"Banished," oil on canvas, 32″ × 28″, 1925.

Alan Stevens Foster

Illustrator, sculptor, cartoonist Alan
Foster was born in Fulton, New York in
1892. During his lifetime he did
illustrations for *Saturday Evening Post,
Colliers, Good Housekeeping, Redbook* and
the *New Yorker.*

"High in Energy—Easily Digested,"
oil on canvas, 30″ × 25″.

Haddon Hubbard Sundblom
1899-1976

Haddon Hubbard Sundblom dominated the art field in Chicago for many years beginning in the 1920's when he formed a studio partnership with Howard Stevens and Edwin Henry.

The studio, under the artistic direction and influence of Sundblom, attracted a great number of young artists who later, as alumni of the "Sundblom circle," went on to become name illustrators in their own right. At one time his studio employed thirty artists.

Sundblom's work was in steady demand for nearly forty years for both magazine stories and advertising campaigns that won him many medals and citations. His style became a hallmark for advertisers such as Procter and Gamble, Colgate, Palmolive, Peet & Company, Cream of Wheat and Maxwell House Coffee.

His portrayal for Coca-Cola of Santa Claus as a jolly, portly figure with twinkling eyes became universally accepted as "the" Santa Claus.

Sundblom also illustrated for calendars and did story illustrations for *The Ladies' Home Journal, Cosmopolitan* and *Good Housekeeping*. Early in his career he created the *"Quaker Man"* picture on boxes of Quaker Oats and the well-known figure of *"Aunt Jemima."*

"She Needs You So," oil on canvas, 29½" × 34½", 1927.
Artist/Agency Fee: $862.50.

H. H. Sundblom

"Energy to Meet,"
oil on canvas, 22″ × 28″, 1924.

Beginning around 1925, Cream of
Wheat changed their style of
advertising. No reference of Cream of
Wheat was made in the painting and
the commercial text was formed around
the illustration as in this example.

"Yes, your baby is growing up," oil on canvas, 22" × 27",
1927. Artist/Agency Fee: $862.50.

H. H. Sundblom

"You Expect Great Things,"
oil on canvas, 40″ × 28″, 1927.
Artist/Agency Fee: $862.50.

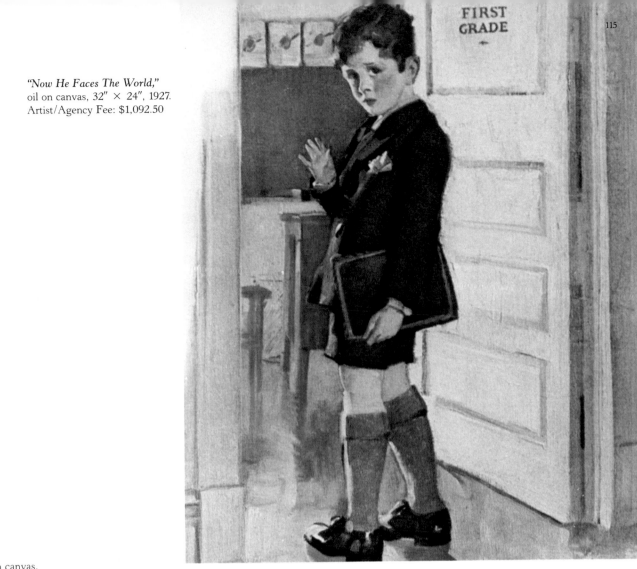

"Now He Faces The World," oil on canvas, 32″ × 24″, 1927. Artist/Agency Fee: $1,092.50

"Already Dreaming," oil on canvas, 19½″ × 36″, 1927. Artist/Agency Fee: $1,092.50

"Ahead of Him,"
oil on canvas, 20″ × 29″, 1927.
Artist/Agency Fee: $1,092.50

"How Little She Understands,"
oil on canvas,
26″ × 24″, 1927.

H. H. Sundblom

"When a Little Girl,"
oil on canvas, 26″ × 23″, 1928.
Artist/Agency Fee: $1,035.

"More Lovable, More Difficult,"
oil on canvas, 31″ × 28″, 1928.
Artist/Agency Fee: $1,035.

"So Unaware of You,"
oil on canvas, 25″ × 22″, 1928.
Artist/Agency Fee: $1,035.

H. H. Sundblom

"When He Begins To Grow,"
oil on canvas, 34″ × 32″, 1928.
Artist/Agency Fee: $1,035.

"Yours—Nothing is too hard," oil on canvas, 27" × 30",
1927. Artist/Agency Fee: $862.50.

"The Clown," oil on canvas, 33″ × 31″, 1928.
Artist/Agency Fee: $1,035.

H. H. Sundblom

"Rules N' Regulations," oil on canvas,
20″ × 33″, 1929.

Andrew Loomis
1892-1959

Loomis was born in Syracuse, New York, and grew up in Zanesville, Ohio. He attended New York's Art Students League and the Chicago Art Institute.

Following the war, Loomis returned to Chicago and eventually opened his own studio as a free-lance artist. Equally at home in either editorial or advertising illustration, Loomis had a long career in both and also painted many outdoor billboards.

His broad experience especially qualified him as a teacher at the American Academy of Art in Chicago. Countless other art students who could not study with him personally have benefited from his several art books. He was the only artist to do portraits of the Dionne quintuplets.

Loomis died in Los Angeles, California in 1959.

"Tom Sawyer,"
oil on board, 44″ × 54″, 1929.
Artist/Agency Fee: $150.

Roy Frederic Spreter

"Bubbling Love of Fun," oil on canvas, 29" × 26", 1929. Artist/Agency Fee: $1,190.

Born in 1899, Spreter is distinguished for the subtlety of his color and values and the good taste which his art conveys to the advertiser's products. He was long associated with the campaigns of Camay, Campbell's Soups, and Bon Ami.

His fiction illustration, equally colorful and artistic, was featured in several women's monthly magazines where his sensitive and beautiful heroines have found much favor.

"The Most Emminent," oil on board, 18″ × 28″, 1929.
Artist/Agency Fee: $1,150.

Harry Anderson
1906-

"Even Pirates Bold," opaque watercolor, 30″ × 25″, 1937.

"The Champ," opaque watercolor, 30″ × 25″, 1937.

Harry Anderson has the distinction of being the only artist still living whose work was commissioned by the Cream of Wheat Company. Born in Chicago, Mr. Anderson attended the University of Illinois and graduated from Syracuse University in 1930. He has had studios successively in New York, Chicago and Washington, D.C. and is currently residing in Ridgefield, Connecticut. A member of the American Water Color Society, he won the Grumbacker Purchase Prize in the 1956 Exhibition.

An allergy to oil paint prompted Anderson to become a water colorist at the onset of his career, however, the development of odorless turpentine several years later allowed him the additional use of oil paints.

Anderson was working at an artist's studio in Chicago during the mid thirties when his work came to the attention of The Cream of Wheat Corporation. As is typical with many artists and their clients today, it was customary for a salesman to represent an artist, presenting samples of his or her work to the client.

During 1937 and 1938 Anderson was employed to do several illustrations for the Cream of Wheat Company. Meeting rush deadlines sometimes permitted him only a few days to complete a painting. He drew young, freckle-faced children engaged in outdoor activity that clearly emphasized the need for a nutritious hot breakfast of Cream of Wheat.

Anderson described himself as a realist, one who is basically unconcerned with technique, but rather paints the world around him as he perceives it.

"Gangway," opaque watercolor, 24″ × 18″, 1937.

H. Anderson

"Gosh All Fishhooks,"
opaque watercolor, 31" × 24", 1938.

Going Down!

"Going Down," opaque watercolor,
25" × 20", 1938.

THE FAMOUS PEOPLE SERIES

She can do anything a boy can

...this little BETTINA BELMONT

Delineator, May, 1930.

Pictorial Review, February, 1930.

JOHN ASPINWALL ROOSEVELT is fortified for the *"strenuous life"* by a care all boys can have

In 1929 and 1930 the Cream of Wheat Company departed from its traditional format of artist illustrated ads with a campaign featuring children of the rich and famous. Combining photographs with spot artwork, these wealthy little spokesmen for Cream of Wheat looked the picture of glowing vitality. The actual engraver's proofs are shown here, to which advertising copy was later added.

MARY *and* ANTOINETTE PINCHOT....

daughters of MR. *and* Mrs. Amos Pinchot *of Park Avenue, New York*

Pictorial Review, December, 1929.

ELIZABETH STUYVESANT FISH

a member of WASHINGTON'S *"youngest set"*

man's Home Companion, October, 1929.

Woman's Home Companion, April, 1930.

Round red cheeks and bright blue eyes for little

CHARLES VAN RENSSELAER, III

His mother starts his daily schedule in a way that specialists advise

Trolley Cards   The last quarter of the nineteenth century saw a bewildering array of inventions that were to change and shape the course of history. The trolley car was one of these, an inexpensive means of transportation that permitted greater mobility for the nation's populace.

"The Ideal Food," oil on canvas, 13″ × 25″, 1922. Unknown artist.

"Makes Babies Grow," oil on canvas, 22″ × 42″, 1922. Artist/Agency Fee: $150. Unknown artist.

The trolley, or street car as it is often called, was a popular means of advertising. Basically miniature posters, trolley cards were placed inside the vehicle, above the passengers' heads. The original artwork shown here was used for trolley cards during the 1920s.

"Summer Favorite," oil on canvas, 22" × 42", 1922. Unknown artist.

"Breakfast, Luncheon, Dessert," oil on board, 11" × 20", 1922. Artist/Agency Fee: $150. Unknown artist.

MEMORABILIA

Salesman's Book. This small, leather bound pad still contained original letters and memos written by a Cream of Wheat Co. salesman. The correspondence, dated 1912, was postmarked Bonners Ferry, Idaho.

When one thinks of Cream of Wheat memorabilia, the most obvious are the hundreds of pictorial, soft-sell magazine ads printed during the first half of this century. Antique shows, flea markets, shops, even a cluttered garage or attic are good sources for old magazines—many of which are no longer in existence. They offer a thoroughly delightful look at the products, fashions and advertising campaigns that mirrored the ever changing lifestyles and attitudes of America.

For advertising collectors, as well as those who simply enjoy fine art, an early Cream of Wheat advertisement evokes a friendly, nostalgic ambience, allowing us the pleasure of owning an "original" without the prohibitive cost.

More difficult to find, but well worth the search, are cloth dolls, cook books, Cream of Wheat sponsored radio premiums, postcards, packing boxes, bowls and more.

For the intrepid and enterprising collector "the fun is in the search," making the discovery of early Cream of Wheat Company promotional materials a rewarding experience. There's a little bit of the archivist in all collectors for whom preserving bits and pieces of the past brings a richer understanding of our consumer heritage.

Cream of Wheat Cook Book, 1899.

CREAM OF WHEAT PREMIUMS.

Send us five of these coupons and 5c to cover postage and we will send you our

DIAMOND COOK BOOK.

Containing about 1,000 new and tested recipes. Or send us ten coupons and 10c and we will send you our beautiful gravure, entitled

"WHEN THE SUN IS LOW."

Size, 18 x 22 inches, mounted on sheet, 26 x 31 inches. This gravure is not a cheap picture, but an elegant art work, which would cost you at any art store in the neighborhood of $5. See miniature copy on the other side of this coupon.

New premiums will be published from time to time, and any of our coupons, one of which will be found in every package of Cream of Wheat, will be received in exchange for either cook books or these pictures.

CREAM OF WHEAT COMPANY,
MINNEAPOLIS, MINN.

Cream of Wheat Cook Book, 1900.

For a period of time beginning around 1899 a coupon was packaged in each box of Cream of Wheat. For five coupons and five cents postage, an individual received the Diamond Cook Book, or for ten coupons and ten cents a choice of a gravure illustration.

136

"*Cream of Wheat Chef Dolls*" were offered in various sizes with minor variations beginning in the 1920's. The more recent doll was issued in 1949. This doll pre-dates the uncut version on the opposite page.

A Few Recipes.

Breakfast Porridge.

To one quart of boiling water add one-half teaspoonful of salt and three-fourths of a cup of CREAM OF WHEAT. Stir in slowly and cook fifteen minutes in a covered dish set in boiling water. Cooking one-half to three-quarters of an hour will not injure, but rather adds to its delicacy. Serve hot with cream and sugar. Many prefer, however, and we think it adds to the daintiness of the dish, that the food be allowed to stand until it assumes a jelly-like consistency before serving.

Pudding.

Heat three cups of milk, to which have been added two well-beaten eggs and a little salt, to nearly boiling. Take about one-half cup of CREAM OF WHEAT and mix well with one cup cold milk till free from lumps; then pour into the hot milk and boil four or five minutes, stirring briskly. Flavor and serve with cream and sugar or pudding sauce.

level full of cocoa, or one teaspoonful of chocolate, moisten with hot water and stir into porridge until it is an even color. Put into a mould. Serve with cream and sugar, vanilla sauce or whipped cream. This is a delicious dessert for those who like the chocolate flavor.

Hot Pudding.

Use above recipe. After cooking as directed turn into an earthen dish and bake in oven about fifteen minutes. Serve hot with hard sauce, lemon sauce, vanilla sauce or milk.

Cranberry Pudding.

Take two cups of hot CREAM OF WHEAT porridge, and one-fourth cup of cranberry juice, with the skins strained out. Stir well and add sugar to taste. Mould and serve with cream and sugar.

Quick Lunch Pudding.

A pint of milk, a little salt and two eggs, well beaten together. Let this come to a boil, then add two tablespoonfuls of CREAM OF WHEAT and cook just five minutes. Flavor and serve hot or cold, as preferred, with cream and sugar.

Children's Diet.

Put one pint of milk in a farina boiler, and when boiling stir in half a cup of CREAM OF WHEAT and half a teaspoonful of salt. Cook steadily for eight or ten minutes. For children or invalids this is very wholesome.

Golden Wheat Pudding.

One quart of milk, three eggs, two-thirds of a cup of CREAM OF WHEAT, and a little salt. To the milk add the yolks of the eggs, well beaten, and allow this to come to a boil; then sprinkle in the CREAM OF WHEAT, stirring slowly meanwhile. Cook about five minutes. Now add the whites of the eggs, beaten to a stiff froth, and remove from fire at once. Flavor to taste and serve with cream and sugar.

Cream of Wheat la Glace.

Put one pint of milk in a farina boiler and heat to boiling point; sweeten, then stir in one-half cup of CREAM OF WHEAT. Cook about ten minutes. Mould in a bowl and when cold slice round in slices about half an inch thick. Lay on a flat dish and put jelly or preserves—jelly preferred—between the slices, terminating with the jelly.

Cream of Wheat. A Dainty Breakfast. This diminutive cook book, only 3¾ inches by 2½ inches, contains recipes such as Cream of Wheat Balls, Cream of Wheat la Glace and Children's Diet.

Cream of Wheat shipping box end.

Magazine advertisements carried information on how to order the *"Cream of Wheat Chef Doll."* A letter addressed to each recipient stated: "Here is the jolly "Cream of Wheat" doll you asked for, ready to be cut, sewed and stuffed. We feel sure this familiar figure will find a hearty welcome from the little folks."

Instructions for completing the doll were printed on the fabric. Also contained in this package was a pamphlet entitled, "Common Sense Feeding Habits For Your Baby." This *"Cream of Wheat Chef Doll"* is one of the last versions to be sold and dates from the late forties.

Buck Rogers skyrocketed into fame in 1928 with his appearance in *"Amazing Stories."* He quickly became a national hero and was popularized in comics, radio and movies, plus countless games and toys for youngsters.

Cream of Wheat sponsored the radio adventures of Buck, his girlfriend Wilma Deering, villain Killer Kane and super scientist Dr. Huer in 1935 and 1936. Captivated youngsters huddled around the radio, eagerly awaiting news of the latest Cream of Wheat premium offer. For only a few boxtops or green triangles from packages of Cream of Wheat, untold hours of fun and fantasy were in the offing. Buck Rogers and Wilma Deering playsuits, medallions, the Buck Rogers secret repeller ray ring, chief explorer badge, disintegrator pistol, solar scout member band, solar scout handbook and a rare set of lead figures by Wm. Britain Ltd. are just a few of the Buck Rogers premiums issued by the Cream of Wheat Co.

The Buck Rogers Solar Scout Handbook was sent to new members of Buck's Solar Scouts. It contained special secrets on how to obtain the elevated position of space ship commander and most importantly, ordering information on all the premiums available from Cream of Wheat. New members pledged "I will eat Cream of Wheat regularly (at least three breakfasts a week) because it gives me the energy I need . . . and because I don't want to disappoint my good friend, Buck Rogers."

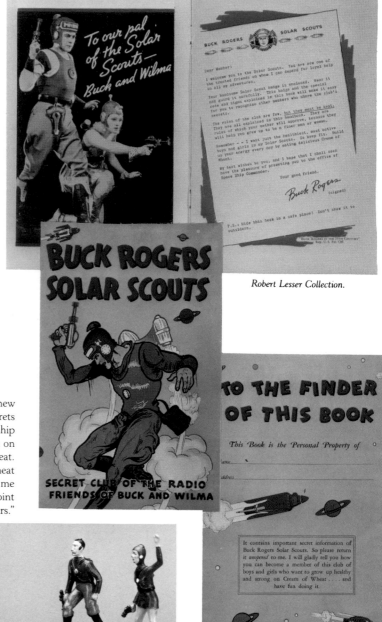

Robert Lesser Collection.

Lead figures by Britains Ltd. The set of six with movable arms: Buck Rogers, Dr. Huer, Ardala, Robot, Wilma, Killer Kane was available for 3 Cream of Wheat box tops and 50 cents. *Photo courtesy Christies East, New York.*

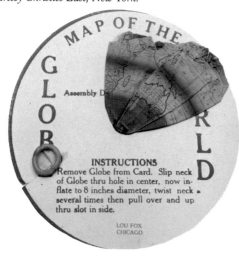

Balloon Globe of the World.

The Solar Scout Member Badge was enclosed along with the handbook to new members of the Buck Rogers Solar Scout Club.

Chief Explorer Badge.

LI'L ABNER. In his popular syndicated strip *"Li'l Abner,"* Al Capp entertained us with a cast of riotously funny hillbilly characters and a plot centered on a "bootiful bowl" of Cream of Wheat. Li'l Abner was a spokesman for Cream of Wheat from 1940 to 1955.

140 Cream of Wheat honored Charles Lindbergh's first nonstop solo transatlantic flight in 1927 with this bowl and its depiction of Lindbergh's plane *"The Spirit of St. Louis."*

SPIRIT OF St. LOUIS

Original zinc engravings *(a device used in letterpress printing into the 1960's)* of Cream of Wheat advertisements. These *"printer's blocks"* were sent free to newspapers to be used in printing ads for local stores.

This recipe book contained such delicious dishes as Snowflake Pudding with Cloth of Gold, Chocolate Blanc Mange and Golden Wheat Pudding. The address listed, 400-404 Third Avenue North, Minneapolis, was the site of the first Cream of Wheat plant in Minneapolis. In 1903 the company had outgrown these facilities and moved to First Avenue North and Fifth Street. The need for a larger and more modern building necessitated another move in 1928 to Stinson Boulevard.

Left:
Cream of Wheat post card, copyright 1910 by the Colonial Art Publishing Co., Brooklyn, N.Y. The reverse side has a blank message space.

Right:
Cream of Wheat advertising card featuring N.C. Wyeth's famous Cream of Wheat painting "Where The Mail Goes Cream of Wheat Goes." The reverse side has an advertising sales message and is dated 1959.

Radio:

Cream of Wheat sponsored the "Let's Pretend" children's radio drama from 1943 until 1952. Known as "radio's outstanding children's theatre," "Let's Pretend" delighted youngsters with tales of witches and goblins, princes and princesses, leprechauns and talking animals.

The show opened with the "Let's Pretend" theme.

Together the cast sang:

Cream of Wheat is so good to eat
Yes we have it every day;
We sing this song, it will make us strong,
And it makes us shout "Hooray!"
It's good for growing babies
And grown-ups too to eat;
For all the family's breakfast
You can't beat Cream of Wheat!

INDEX